Imagine losing your mother, your father, and your home in a matter of months. What would you do? This is precisely what happened to Esther, and in this book, Charis McRoy uses her imagination to explore what Esther might have been thinking, feeling, and experiencing using the words of a young girl pouring out her heart in her diary. Whether she was living as a street orphan, moving in with her cousin Mordecai and his wife, Chana, or winning the ultimate beauty pageant making her queen of all Persia, Esther holds on to her faith, recording it all in her treasured diary.

Naturally, the author's imagination has filled in some of the blanks left in the biblical account. Nevertheless, the storyline remains faithful to the history that we do know. As you read, you will admire anew a young woman's determination to be faithful to the God who was always faithful to her, even amid trying circumstances.

THE STAR
A PEEK INSIDE ESTHER'S DIARY

CHARIS McROY

TEACH Services, Inc.
PUBLISHING
www.TEACHServices.com • (800) 367-1844

World rights reserved. This book or any portion thereof may not be copied or reproduced in any form or manner whatever, except as provided by law, without the written permission of the publisher, except by a reviewer who may quote brief passages in a review.

The author assumes full responsibility for the accuracy and interpretation of the Ellen White quotations cited in this book. Unless otherwise indicated, all scripture quotations are taken from the King James Version of the Bible.

The ESV® Bible (The Holy Bible, English Standard Version®). ESV® Text Edition: 2016. Copyright © 2001 by Crossway, a publishing ministry of Good News Publishers. The ESV® text has been reproduced in cooperation with and by permission of Good News Publishers. Unauthorized reproduction of this publication is prohibited. All rights reserved.

Copyright © 2019 Charis McRoy
Copyright © 2019 TEACH Services, Inc.
ISBN-13: 978-1-4796-0985-7 (Paperback)
ISBN-13: 978-1-4796-0986-4 (ePub)
Library of Congress Control Number: 2019931098

Scripture quotations marked The Message are taken from The Message. Copyright © 1993, 1994, 1995, 1996, 2000, 2001, 2002. Used by permission of NavPress Publishing Group.

Scripture quotations marked NASB are taken from the New American Standard Bible®, copyright © 1960, 1962, 1963, 1968, 1971, 1972, 1973, 1975, 1977, 1995 by The Lockman Foundation. Used by permission.

Scripture quotations marked NIV are taken from The Holy Bible, New International Version®, NIV®. Copyright © 1973, 1978, 1984, 2011 by Biblica, Inc.TM Used by permission. All rights reservedworldwide.

Texts credited to NKJV are taken from the New King James Version®. Copyright © 1982 by Thomas Nelson, Inc. Used by permission. All rights reserved.

Scripture quotations marked NLT are taken from the Holy Bible, New Living Translation, copyright © 1996, 2004, 2007 by Tyndale House Foundation. Used by permission of Tyndale House Publishers, Inc., Carol Stream, Illinois 60188. All rights reserved.

Scripture quotations marked REB are taken from The Revised English Bible, copyright © Cambridge University Press and Oxford University Press 1989. All rights reserved.

TEACH Services, Inc.
PUBLISHING
www.TEACHServices.com • (800) 367-1844

Dedicated to:

Mom, Dad, Malachi, and Royal.
May the Lord continue to bless each one of you.
Thanks for your love and support.

Acknowledgements

Special thanks to:

The Lord Almighty. Thank you for giving me this wonderful idea to use my talent to -glorify your name.

> 1ˢᵗ day of Nissan
> In the year of Jehovah
> During the reign of King Xerxes

Dear Diary,

I feel quite sad right now. Ever since Mama died, life has not been quite the same. I know it has been nearly two years since she died, but my heart is still wrenched in two.

To complicate things, Father is now very ill. I have done everything I can to help him, but he only seems to get worse.

Oftentimes I stay up all night, for I cannot sleep. I toss and turn on my mat, and wake up tired and even more anxious. I worry deeply about him, and it troubles me to think about his suffering.

I must go now, for my dear father is writhing in pain. I have to tend to him immediately.

Sincerely,

Hadassah

The Star: A Peek Inside Esther's Diary

3rd day of Nissan
In the year of Jehovah
During the reign of King Xerxes

Dear Diary,

I sent a messenger to summon the village doctor, because Father has grown even worse. Now he is even paler, and his fever has rapidly risen.

When the doctor arrived, he hurriedly took out his instruments and began to examine my father. I heard him mumbling to himself, as if he was deeply trying to think. Then after trying to find the cause for Father's illness and the medicine to treat it, he finally gave up.

After a pause, our eyes met. Then he broke the news that I was really dreading. He sadly told me, "I'm afraid your father has only a few days left."

I instantly begged him to tell me if anything could be done, but the doctor just shook his head. The answer was no.

Oh, if only Jehovah would outstretch His mighty hand, and heal my beloved father!

Sincerely,

Hadassah

> 5th day of Nissan
> In the year of Jehovah
> During the reign of King Xerxes

Dear Diary,

Today when I arose to check on Father, a dreaded sight met my eyes.

He lay on his bed, motionless and pale. I nervously went forward to check his pulse. However, there was none. He is dead.

I cannot bear the thought that his strong arms that always wrapped around me in love will never embrace me again. Now I am all alone with no one to love me. I am covered in a thick blanket of sadness. How I grieve over my loss, but Jehovah's will has been done.

> *I am covered in a thick blanket of sadness*

Sincerely,

Hadassah

8th day of Nissan
In the year of Jehovah
During the reign of King Xerxes

Dear Diary,

I am at home sitting by the fire as I write. I have been out of the house all day, so when I got home I immediately changed into work clothes, and grabbed my gardening tools.

I gathered some potatoes and carrots from the garden and went to the shed to get some dried fish to fix a simple supper for Dan, my puppy, and myself.

While I wait for the stew, I decided to write a little to ease my mind.

Today was Father's funeral. Several of his fellow workers at the blacksmith shop were kind to attend the service. A couple of the villagers who had known him also came.

Old Mark, the farmer who was like a grandfather to me, showed up, too. Despite his crippled leg, he came faithfully to support me. My sister-like friend, Alzbeta, came with her mother. I managed to crack a little smile, when I spotted my adventurous and mischievous companion. Having my close friends at the funeral really encouraged me and helped improve my day.

Sincerely,

Hadassah

9th day of Nissan
In the year of Jehovah
During the reign of King Xerxes

Dear Diary,

I never imagined life like this. My emptiness is inexpressible and the pain unbearable. Mother's dead, and now Father. My older brother is so caught up with his new wife that he doesn't care a bit about me.

I remember the day quite well when the landlord came by to inform me that I had to move out because my father was in debt. But Father was dead, and I am just a child, so what was I supposed to do about it? The man even threatened to enslave me to pay back his debt!

Oh, well. It is what it is, and I have to face it.

Sincerely,

Hadassah

10th day of Nissan
In the year of Jehovah
During the reign of King Xerxes

Dear Diary,

Today, I met the snobbiest girl ever! It is already bad enough to hear the snickers of girls passing by on their way to draw water from the well or the old ladies that look down their noses in disgust.

But there was something different about this girl. She was with a group of friends, probably as snobby as she was. She came up close to me and shoved a beautiful handkerchief in my face and said loudly, "I bet a lazy girl like you will never be able to afford something like this!"

She turned around to her group of friends and they all started laughing at me, pointing at my worn clothing. Then they walked away. I have never felt so humiliated.

Sincerely,

Hadassah

12th day of Nissan
In the year of Jehovah
During the reign of King Xerxes

Dear Diary,

Today, I felt so alone. I went to the synagogue, since it is Shabbat. I nearly cried when I remembered the days when Mother, Father, my brother, and I would go to the synagogue together. But now things have changed, and I go by myself. Even though my brother still lives in the area, I never see him at the synagogue. I don't think he practices Judaism anymore now that he is with that Persian wife of his. I wish things could be the same. Why is it that everyone else has a family except for me?

Even around my own people I am not welcomed, because I am poor. They usually sit far away from me and never greet me like they do the other children. I don't smell bad, if that is what they are afraid of. (I always make sure to take a bath at the river, especially on Friday nights and I wear my best clothing.) You would think that since we are Jehovah's people we would treat each other differently, but we don't do any better than the heathens around us.

Finally, I just couldn't take it anymore, and I left early, right before the rabbi got up to speak. I can imagine the stares I received as I hastily made my way out of the synagogue, but I didn't care. I ran all the way back home. I huddled in my dwelling and just cried and cried as the rain pounded on the roof. I tried to soothe myself with the songs my mother often sang to me, but that just made me cry even more.

Anger and sadness started to build up. Why did both of my parents have to die? Why did my own remaining relatives have to be so unsympathetic? Why are some people so mean?

Sincerely,
Hadassah

The Star: A Peek Inside Esther's Diary

> 13ᵗʰ day of Nissan
> In the year of Jehovah
> During the reign of King Xerxes

Dear Diary,

Today, I talked with one of the farmers that often comes to the market. When my late grandfather lived with us, he would come over to play marbles sometimes, and then he also appeared at Mother's funeral. He seemed to be a nice man and would always bring my brother and me a freshly picked plum from his farm.

When he saw me, he smiled and came over to see me. We talked for a little while. Before he left, he reached into a knapsack and brought out a few items: a few coins, a small loaf of bread, a blanket, and sure enough—a plum. He told me that he wished he could help me more, but he was already caring for his orphaned granddaughters who were not yet three years of age. I just gratefully told him, "Thank you so much, sir! May Jehovah bless you!"

> *No one wanted a little child to work for them*

Then he told me, "Don't call me sir, you can call me Sabba—grandfather." With that he hobbled away.

Today, I decided to try looking for work again. I have looked for work in the past, but no one wanted to be bothered. I went to several business owners' homes asking for work, but usually they would just slam the door in my face before I even spoke a word. It was clear: no one wanted a little child to work for them.

But fortunately, one kind woman answered the door when I knocked. She sort of reminded me of my great-aunt: extremely curly hair and big brown eyes. Only, this woman was much nicer. She invited me into her humble mud home, seated me on a wooden stool and gave me a cup of cool water. I learned that her name was Aniko, but she was affectionately called Aunt Niko by everyone who knew her.

She told me that for a long while she had looked for someone to help her operate her bakery, so I eagerly told her that I would be willing to help her. She told me that she would love for me to work with her, and she would also pay me! I was overjoyed.

I start tomorrow early in the morning. Although I will have to work basically all day, I will be able to buy food!

Sincerely,

Hadassah

The Star: A Peek Inside Esther's Diary

> 7th day of Iyyar
> In the year of Jehovah
> During the reign of King Xerxes

Dear Diary,

Aunt Niko gave me some coins today for helping her bake. I am thankful to have some money now. But unfortunately, I don't have a lot of food left. I have been selling most of the crops in the garden, and have eaten most of the dried fish. But thanks to Aunt Niko, I had some bread to eat with it.

I have received only fifty shekels and a bekah, which is just a third of what I owe to my father's debtors. I have a few necessary purchases to make, so I will have even less to contribute to paying for my father's debts. I hope God will supply my needs according to His will!

Sincerely,

Hadassah

The Star: A Peek Inside Esther's Diary ◆ 19

16th day of Iyyar
In the year of Jehovah
During the reign of King Xerxes

Dear Diary,

Today I went to the synagogue. When it was time to present offering to the Lord, I felt an urge to give something. Although I didn't have much left now, only ten shekels, I decided to give it to Jehovah. I have learned to trust in the Lord, and put my faith in Him.

Despite the fact that it was all I had left, I believe God will supply my needs. I sure hope He does, before I am forced to leave the only home I have known.

When I came back home, I went to the garden. Resting beneath my favorite fig tree filled me with a sense of peace. For the rest of the afternoon I spent time talking to Jehovah. It reminded me of the special times Father and I used to spend together on Yom Shabbat, but only better.

Sincerely,
Hadassah

The Star: A Peek Inside Esther's Diary

>20th day of Iyyar
>In the year of Jehovah
>During the reign of King Xerxes

Dear Diary,

I was on my way back home from Aunt Niko's bakery when I heard a distressed squeal nearby. As an animal lover, I went to investigate to see the cause of the sound. Following the sound, I came across a horse that was apparently injured. Its leg had a serious bruise that needed treatment right away. She had a halter on, so she must have had an owner before. I think that she was abandoned once she got hurt.

I immediately set down my bag, and started searching for some herbs. I found a good number of herbs and then created a poultice to put on the horse's wound. I talked to her reassuringly as I swabbed the mixture on her leg.

Soon she gained enough strength, and I led her down the road to my home. I settled her down in the barn, which had once housed several cows but now was empty.

I then ran to the fields, and plucked up some oats and placed them in bag. When I returned, the horse gratefully ate all the oats that I fed her. She was content and fell asleep. I decided to name her Missy.

Jehovah has provided me with another animal friend. I thank Him dearly for blessing me so abundantly!

Sincerely,

Hadassah

24ᵗʰ day of Iyyar
In the year of Jehovah
During the reign of King Xerxes

Dear Diary,

Missy is healing quite nicely. Her leg is almost better. I took her outside for a little walk along with my dog, Dan. She first walked at a steady pace with Dan and me, and then began to trot a little bit. I ran after her and tried to get her to slow down. It makes me happy to see her doing much better. Soon, I will be able to ride her.

I told Missy and Dan goodnight and went inside the hut.

I know it is past my bedtime, but I thought I would just write for a little while, since I usually don't get to write much anymore because of work. My eyelids are slowly drooping and my body will not permit me to write anymore.

Sincerely,

Hadassah

27th day of Iyyar
In the year of Jehovah
During the reign of King Xerxes

Dear Diary,

This morning as I was helping Aunt Niko roll some dough into flat loaves of bread, she told me something that made me sad. She said she is moving away to another town, which means she will be closing her bakery. I will miss her dearly, for she and I have developed a friendship during the time we have known each other. It also means that I will have to find another job as soon as I can unless the Lord works another miracle.

Sincerely,

Hadassah

The Star: A Peek Inside Esther's Diary ◆ 23

6th day of Sivan
In the year of Jehovah
During the reign of King Xerxes

Dear Diary,

I still haven't been successful in finding another job these last few days, except for washing clothes for the neighbors. Most people wash their own clothes, which leaves me with few customers.

I am trying my best to ration out my dwindling supply of food, but soon the vegetables and fish will be gone. I am trying my best to save as much money as possible, but I cannot avoid buying necessary things.

It breaks my heart to do so, but I have sold a few of Mother's and Father's things in order to earn a few shekels. I sold Father's best pair of sandals, his whittling knife, and favorite chair. I also sold Mother's pretty vase that had once belonged to her great-grandmother.

Each and every day, I am dependent on God

Each and every day, I am dependent on God. The little bits of food that I eat do not fill me, but the Lord has kept me from starving. Jehovah also provides for my animals. Although they don't have much to eat either, they are still doing well.

I hope that Jehovah gives me the money, or somehow intervenes in this situation.

Sincerely,

Hadassah

8th day of Sivan
In the year of Jehovah
During the reign of King Xerxes

Dear Diary,

Today is truly my lucky day! For now I will have a true home, and a family to love. You may be wondering how this happened, so let me explain.

As I was busy sweeping the floor, Dan furiously wagged his tail, and bounded back and forth across the hut. I know that he only does that when he really gets excited, and sees something or someone he loves.

Because nothing good has happened around here for a long time, I left my straw broom and followed him to the door. When I swung open the door, I saw my cousin, Mordecai!

My heart bounded for joy. I eagerly ran to meet him, with Dan on my heels.

"Mordecai!" I exclaimed. "You are really here! I never imagined that you would come here!"

The two of us embraced, and Mordecai spun me around. I giggled so much, something I haven't done in such a long time.

Then he gingerly set me down on the ground. He began, "Hadassah, I understand that your mother and father have passed away."

I nodded.

After taking a deep breath he continued, "How would you like to come and live with me in Susa?"

I eagerly told him that I would love to. I hurried inside, grabbed some clothes, my diary, quill and ink, and packed them into a small goatskin bag. Then running to the barn, I grabbed my horse, Missy, and mounted her. I whistled to Dan, and he came trotting beside the horse. Then together, Mordecai and I started the journey to his house.

Along the way Mordecai and I talked together. I asked him many things about the city of Susa and about his job as an officer for the king.

Now here I am safe and sound with my cousin. We are beside a creek resting from traveling all day in the hot sun. Even my usually energetic dog is panting like crazy. Mordecai says we will spend the night here, and then continue our journey tomorrow.

I am very grateful to God for answering my prayers. Jehovah is truly incredible. Well, it is almost dark, and soon I will not be able to see to write.

I bid you goodnight.

Sincerely,

Hadassah

12th day of Sivan
In the year of Jehovah
During the reign of King Xerxes

Dear Diary,

We have finally arrived at Mordecai's house. It is very extravagant and richly decorated! I know it is nothing compared to the king's palace, but it is truly amazing to me, as a girl who lived in a simple hut.

As soon as we set foot on the threshold, Mordecai's beautiful and kind wife, Chana, came to greet us. Behind Chana, I saw two chubby faces peeking from behind her long skirt. Chana laughed.

"These are your younger cousins, Earin and Adlai."

She tried to coax the little toddlers to come and say hello, but they backed away and hid even more behind their mother. I smiled. I heard the back door slam. Then I saw a boy around my age appear in the hallway. He joined his mother and little brothers. His name is Benjamin, her eldest son.

When we entered, deliciously tempting smells awaited us. Then I saw servants carrying huge platters of rich cakes, fruits, and meat. It looked almost too good to eat! However, once I sat at the table, I quickly consumed the delicacies placed before me, satisfying my hunger pangs.

> *...but it will be Esther, for it means 'star'*

One of the servants noticed my dog Dan, who was quite hungry. So he went to the kitchen, and hurried back with a small bowl of meat and rice. Dan was very happy to have some food. He ate every last bite in his dish.

As we were enjoying dinner, Mordecai said to me, "Before I came to your home to bring you here to live with us, Chana and I have decided to give you a new name. No longer will it be Hadassah, but it will be Esther, for it means 'star.' After all, you have a brilliant smile! We both agreed it was a fitting name for you."

Chana nodded in agreement. I just simply beamed.

Soon after supper there were more surprises awaiting me. Chana brought me upstairs and led me to her room. She then presented me with a new robe.

"Take off that old garment that you have on. Instead, put this one on; this is fit for a star! It was my daughter's, and it fit her beautifully."

She wiped a tear from her eye, but then warmly smiled as I threw my tattered dress to the ground, and put on the beautiful robe in its place.

Then she led me along another corridor and escorted me to my new bedroom. I gasped in surprise, as I looked around my room. It was more than I would have ever even imagined!

On the floor was a soft deerskin mat with rich wool blankets, instead of the straw mat I had before. I even had a small desk and bench against one wall. The walls were painted in brilliant colors. I also had a small vase of daisies on a decorative table. Everything was just simply beautiful.

I thank Jehovah for blessing me so graciously and for a family who loves me dearly.

Sincerely,

Esther

The Star: A Peek Inside Esther's Diary

14th day of Sivan
In the year of Jehovah
During the reign of King Xerxes

Dear Diary,

Today I woke up at dawn. Mordecai said that he wanted to take me to the palace to see what his work is like. I agreed. I quickly learned that he was very busy.

Often other court officials would stop in and talk to Mordecai for long periods of time. He was also very busy collecting information, and most importantly, writing. The king would often ask him to write reports concerning major events throughout the region. When I read the reports, I learned quite a bit about life outside our city.

Finally, after writing nearly all morning, his pen stopped. He told us that it was time to take a break. I was quite relieved, because my legs had gotten a cramp, and I was just simply bored. All morning, I was looking for something to do, from trying to count the hundreds of clay tablets around me to the one defect in the seemingly perfect floor beams.

As I skipped down the hall with my cousin, one of the ladies of the court scowled at the sound of my clip-clopping along the marble floor.

From experience in a village with strict elderly women, I have learned that you should take a hint to stop doing something when you are given the "evil eye." So I stopped skipping. I really wish that ladies could have a little fun every once in a while!

I am going to eat with my cousin and some other court officials. I will write later. If they see me writing, they will consider it a disgrace for me to be literate, because I am a girl. I am definitely not in the mood for any more evil eyes!

Sincerely,
Esther

The Star: A Peek Inside Esther's Diary ◆ 29

15th day of Sivan
In the year of Jehovah
During the reign of King Xerxes

Dear Diary,

I went with Mordecai again to the palace, since Chana went to another town to help deliver a baby, and pretty much everyone else was out and about. Today he said we would not be staying very long at the court. I silently cheered to myself. What a relief. As I sat down, Mordecai began to read some of the reports gathered from nearby cities in the region and take notes. I sat there watching him as he skillfully wrote on the clay tablets.

After a while, he asked me if I would like to try. I scampered over to his desk, and sat next to him. He showed me how to use a stick called a stylus to make markings in the moist clay and then use a wax seal to make it official. He then handed me a small clay tablet and a sharp stylus. I then got to work writing on the tablet. I actually found it quite enjoyable. When I finished writing, I presented him my completed message.

He exclaimed, "Esther, this is excellent! Good job. Maybe one day I could use you to help me copy some reports. You would make a good scribe!" he chuckled and ruffled my long brown curls.

"I would love to, Cousin Mordecai!" I responded. Then I slid off the bench and went over to the bin of clay tablets, and started writing on another tablet.

All too soon Mordecai said, "It is time to go home now, little star. It is about time we have some fun."

On our way back towards the house, we bumped into Alzbeta! What a pleasant surprise. I haven't seen her since Father's funeral. I happily went over to her and greeted her. Soon our little chatter grew into a lively conversation. Mordecai then spoke up.

"Since I see you two are enjoying yourselves, Esther, I suppose you can spend a little time with your friend before we go home."

I thanked Mordecai and continued talking with my friend. Then we raced with one another over a hill that was close by. During our conversation, I learned that her family had moved to the area. After a time, Alzbeta announced that she must be on her way home. We said goodbye to one another, and then Alzbeta bounded away.

> *I'm sure God will have a plan for your life and cause you to greatly succeed*

As Mordecai and I started back home he asked how I enjoyed myself. Of course my response was that I had a fabulous time.

Then he said jokingly, "I wish I could play around with my friends every once in a while." But then thoughtfully he added, "As an adult I now have more responsibilities and with that comes a lot of work. One day, Esther, you will grow up and have a job to do. Whatever that job might be, I'm sure God will have a plan for your life and cause you to greatly succeed."

I thought quietly for a moment as I gazed up into the starry night sky. Could Mordecai be right about God having a plan for me? I guess I will just have to wait and see for myself.

Sincerely,

Esther

17th day of Sivan
In the year of Jehovah
During the reign of King Xerxes

Dear Diary,

This morning Chana came home. She looked quite exhausted, but she greeted me happily. She told of the things that had happened in the past couple of days. The first disaster that happened was that the mother had difficulties giving birth, which could have meant danger to both her and the baby.

After giving birth, the child did not seem to be too well. He refused to drink milk at first, but Chana had stayed up day and night tending to the child. Finally he drank and regained his strength.

After breakfast Mordecai and I set off to the palace courts. There we spent the day. Mordecai was true to his promise, and allowed me to help him copy some reports. I thought my work looked rather pitiful, but he congratulated me on the seemingly fine work I had done.

Well, I better stop writing because Chana is calling me downstairs to set the table for dinner. Goodbye for now.

Sincerely,

Esther

The Star: A Peek Inside Esther's Diary

> 19th day of Sivan
> In the year of Jehovah
> During the reign of King Xerxes

Dear Diary,

Mordecai, the whole family, and I went to the synagogue today. On our way, we stopped by Alzbeta's house to pick her up since her mother was sick and her dad was out of town.

When we arrived the only seats available were near the back of the synagogue next to a massive stone column. I tried my best to listen to the rabbi, but I couldn't focus very well. I almost fell asleep, but reminded myself that I was in the Lord's house and should be reverent and listen to His words.

After the service, we solemnly bowed our heads in prayer to the Lord, and then we were dismissed. We held hands to avoid us getting separated in the sea of people.

We walked home to eat lunch. After lunch, Mordecai took us out to the rose garden, and read us stories from the ancient scrolls. For the rest of the evening, we all enjoyed communion with Jehovah. Mordecai later took Alzbeta home. I will write later.

Sincerely,

Esther

The Star: A Peek Inside Esther's Diary ◆ 33

Two years later ...
1st day of Tammuz
In the year of Jehovah
During the third year in the reign of King Xerxes

Dear Diary,

Mordecai attended a banquet today. The king invited all his nobles, servants, and princes. This feast is 180 days long! I thought that was quite a long time to party. It started in Nissan and will end in Elul. Mordecai did not wish to attend all of the banquets, but he decided to go today.

When he came home, he told me about it. The king had displayed all his wealth and splendor before his royal subjects. Most of the items were gold, and very expensive and exquisite. They also ate, drank, and laughed together. The place was splendidly decorated with all of the finest ornaments that all of Persia could offer.

I think I would enjoy going to such a luxurious feast if I were ever invited!

Sincerely,

Esther

8th day of Tammuz
In the year of Jehovah
During the third year in the reign of King Xerxes

Dear Diary,

A messenger came to our courtyard bringing the news of the king's banquet, which is to last for a week and starts tonight! He also told Chana that there is a feast for the women, which is held by Queen Vashti. I wonder just how many parties King Xerxes plans to have! With all these parties, there will be so much fun but little work that is getting done.

> *There were fancy couches composed of genuine gold and shiny silver*

The messenger told us that this party is going to be held in the palace garden, but he did not provide any more information.

We all hastily started to get ready for this special occasion. I put on a silky pink dress, an elegant scarlet shawl, and my golden slippers.

As soon as everyone was ready, Mordecai hitched the horses to the wagon, and we started along the dirt road. There were many people, all on their way to the feast. The clopping hooves of horses, and thumping feet, created huge clouds of dust.

After we found a spot on the hill among the many other carts, wagons, and horses, we walked on the cobblestone path that wound its way to the garden. Vashti's quarters were just beyond the garden, but before heading over there, we looked around to see what the garden was like. Walking amongst the noisy crowds, hearing the singing, and watching the dancing was somewhat like market day. Like the market, there were many interesting sights and smells to take in.

The garden was simply beautiful. The servants must have worked very hard to create such an inviting scene. The pavement of the garden walkways consisted of red, blue, white, and black marble. There were fancy couches composed of genuine gold and shiny silver. Around the borders of this magnificent garden were green, white, and blue curtains attached to pillars.

The garden was so beautiful that I wished we didn't have to leave, but Chana dragged me along to the queen's banquet, while Mordecai attended his feast.

As we were riding along in the wagon in the evening, Mordecai told Chana and me about the feast he attended. He said that when it was time to eat, they were seated around a table with beautiful silverware, and were each given unique cups and glasses. Everyone received a different kind!

The food was also very elegantly and royally presented. They were served pastries, cakes, and other rich foods. Bread and large portions of meat were in abundance. While the people ate, a dancer entertained them with her enchanting performance. Everyone was pleased, and even the king offered his pleasant remarks.

Whatever else he said, I do not know because I closed my eyes and dozed off to sleep. When I felt a jerk as we came across the gravel that led to the barn, I knew that we were at home. I rubbed my eyes and slowly walked inside. Before I plopped straight on my mat, I decided that I would write tonight. I am very exhausted, so I bid you goodnight.

Sincerely,
Esther

14th day of Tammuz
In the year of Jehovah
During the third year in the reign of King Xerxes

Dear Diary,

Mordecai went to the banquet today, but Chana stayed behind.

It is the last day of the feast, so today is extra special. The king was quite intoxicated from consuming all the wine over this past week. Out of his delirium, he summoned his wife, Vashti, to come in wearing her royal crown, so that all the people with him could see her beauty. The chamberlains were commanded to bring her into his presence.

When they arrived at the queen's home and implored Vashti to appear before King Xerxes, she refused. The servants dismally returned to the king with the disturbing news. When King Xerxes heard that his gorgeous queen had refused to obey his orders, his anger was kindled, and he was quite furious. The music ceased, and the people became quiet. They murmured among themselves about the king's unhappy disposition.

According the Medo-Persian laws, a king's orders must not be disobeyed, unless you desired to be punished. The king gathered his officials together to find out what advice they had to offer concerning what should be done to Queen Vashti, since she disobeyed the king's command.

From the advice given to him by his servants, he decided to send a decree throughout the land summoning wives to respect their husbands and obey them, to make sure that wives never disobeyed like Vashti. He also banished Vashti from her beautiful home, and ruled that she could never return into his presence.

What a humiliating day it must have been for Vashti, since she must leave her riches behind.

I wonder who will replace Queen Vashti and take her position. What a sad ending of a once happy feast.

Sincerely,

Esther

> Three years later ...
> 4th day of Av
> In the year of Jehovah
> During the sixth year in the reign of King Xerxes

Dear Diary,

Today I stayed home with Chana. I helped her cook. We were expecting to have guests tonight. I also had my sewing lessons. I really despise sewing, but Chana says that this will be an important skill when I am married.

Although I don't enjoy doing housework, spending time with Chana is something I really enjoy doing.

I must quickly get back to work because the guests will soon be here.

Sincerely,

Esther

> 10th day of Av
> In the year of Jehovah
> During the sixth year in the reign of King Xerxes

Dear Diary,

Today was very interesting. I had another sewing lesson. As I was working, Chana told me that I was beginning to look more and more like a young lady. She said it makes her happy to see how I am growing up, and that very soon, I will get married and have a family of my own!

The idea of getting married made me shudder. I am only fifteen, but in a couple of years, I will be around the age of being given into marriage.

I especially don't like the fact that one day I will go off and get married and leave Mordecai and Chana. It makes me sad that I will leave the people that have been like parents to me. It has been several years since I have lived with them now and it has just been wonderful. They have been a true blessing to me.

Sincerely,

Esther

12th day of Av
In the year of Jehovah
During the sixth year of the reign of King Xerxes

Dear Diary,

Today is finally Yom Shabbat! I always look forward to celebrating the Lord's holy Shabbat. Today, Chana, Earin, my younger cousin, and I went to the synagogue since the others are away on a trip.

The synagogue wasn't as packed as before, since another one has opened up nearby. The rabbi read to us the accounts of David. Time after time, I was reminded of God's faithfulness to His people. While Saul was seeking to harm David, God protected him and supplied his needs. He gave him food to eat and safe places to take refuge in. God was faithful to David, and David was faithful to God. Although there were times when he made mistakes, he mostly stayed true to God. He often praised the Lord for His goodness and mercy. He was kind to his enemy, and even turned down opportunities in which he could have killed his adversary. I hope that I can be that close to God like David was.

Sincerely,
Esther

> *I always look forward to celebrating the Lord's holy Shabbat*

15th day of Av
In the year of Jehovah
During the sixth year in the reign of King Xerxes

Dear Diary,

What a busy day I had today! Since Mordecai has come back from his business trip to Ethiopia, he has not been feeling well. I went with Chana to the market to pick up some herbs to make some tea for him. We then picked up some material from Lady Margarete, who is the best seamstress in town. We picked some apples, and made preserves and pastries, and baked several of loaves of bread.

After supper I took care of Missy and her week-old foal, Charlotte. As I groomed Missy and Charlotte, I shared with them the things that were on my mind. I told them of Mordecai being sick, and of the busy day I have had. Thinking that I was not being heard by anyone except the horses, I kept talking. Soon I realized that I wasn't alone. Chana was right behind me! When I turned around, I nearly shrieked in surprise.

She thanked me for all my hard work and encouraged me to go inside with her. Once inside, I slumped onto my mat and took a long, satisfying nap. Once I woke up, I felt much better and much rested. I went to inquire about Mordecai to see if he was feeling better. Chana informed me he is feeling much better. Jehovah be praised!

I will write later.

Sincerely,
Esther

20th day of Av
In the year of Jehovah
During the sixth year of the reign of King Xerxes

Dear Diary,

I saw my friend Alzbeta today near the marketplace. It has been a while since I have seen her. We talked about what our lives were like, and among other things, we talked of our dreams of growing up.

I listened intently as she explained how her family had adopted the culture of the Persians and now worshipped other gods including Ashtoreth. However, despite her family's poor choices, she decided that she would not partake in any of it. As a result, it has caused strife in her family. Her mother has tried so earnestly to discourage her from attending meetings in the synagogue and observing the holy Sabbath. Her father has even threatened to disown her if she continues to worship Jehovah.

I put my arm around her as she wept and suggested that perhaps she could stay with us. When I arrived at my home and met Chana, I talked with her at once about Alzbeta's predicament. She agreed to have her stay for a little while.

I am writing in the dim light of my candle. I am so glad Chana agreed to have Alzbeta stay with us. God be praised for His awesome works! I'm getting sleepy now, so farewell.

Sincerely,
Esther

21st day of Av
In the year of Jehovah
During the sixth year in the reign of King Xerxes

Dear Diary,

Alzbeta is now living with us. Today I took her to see Charlotte the foal. When I opened the creaky wooden door and we walked inside, she was excited to see her. Alzbeta reached over to stroke Charlotte's beautiful chestnut mane.

She was curious to find out why Charlotte and her mother are in the carpenter's shed and not the barn. I explained that Mordecai's barn is already teeming with horses, and that other mares can be quite aggressive at times. Missy is frail now and she and the baby can rest quietly together there.

We picked the prettiest roses and daffodils that were in sight as we walked through the garden and ran with the wind throughout our serene environment. Each of us was enveloped in a world of our own, each filled with happiness and enjoyment.

Finally, leaving the beauty of creation behind, we once again returned to the house—back to work grinding corn into flour. The beat of the large pole as it crushed the corn was so rhythmic, unlike being outdoors. In the outdoors, the beat doesn't always have to be the same; it can be whatever you want it to be.

I cast my thoughts aside and continued crushing the grain in the huge clay pot. Finally, the pounding could cease. My arms ached so much from this grinding, but I enjoyed this work and spending time with Alzbeta.

I stretched and then slumped unto a chair, very exhausted. Before I knew it, the clank of dishes in the kitchen and the sweet smells that filled the air told me that lunch was ready.

I instantly burst into the kitchen, and sat in my spot. Alzbeta followed closely behind. Soon the servants arrived carrying the food. Afterwards, Chana told us that we should spend a little time sewing. Reluctantly, Alzbeta and I went upstairs to fetch our thread, needles, and other necessary supplies. We are like one another in some ways. We both detest sewing.

Today has been quite filled with activities, but it feels wonderful. I'm certain that Alzbeta would say the same thing.

Farewell. I must write later. I have to get ready for a meeting at the synagogue.

Sincerely,

Esther

The Star: A Peek Inside Esther's Diary

7th day of, Tevet
In the year of Jehovah
During the sixth year in the reign of King Xerxes

Dear Diary,

Today a courier came to our home while Alzbeta and I were busy sewing some new dresses. I rushed to answer the door. He carried in his hand a letter from the king asking for every young virgin to appear at the king's house. So we dropped our needles and said goodbye to Mordecai and Chana. Before I left, Mordecai whispered in my ear, "Don't tell anyone that you are a Jew."

I promised that I wouldn't and set out the door with Alzbeta. We were then hurriedly escorted into a horse-drawn carriage along with other girls and went off to the king's palace. When we arrived, we were led inside by Hegai, who was in charge of the women. He was stunned by my appearance, and kept staring at me in surprise. His gaze made me feel quite jittery from my head to my toes. He then escorted me to the finest rooms in the women's house.

> *Don't tell anyone that you are a Jew*

The main room was quite similar to mine at home, so I felt a little more at ease. There were also rooms for the maidens, a closet, and a spa chamber. The colors were bright and some of the furniture was made of gold or silver! The bed was carved out of ivory and coated with gold. I noticed that several of the shelves were crammed with all kinds of beauty mixtures! There were sweet perfumes, herbal oils, and myrrh.

Just as I was beginning to relax, there was a loud thump on the door. It was Hegai. Butterflies entered my stomach again, and I struggled to swallow my tenseness. He announced that tomorrow we would begin my beauty treatments. To make sure we are ready to be seen by the king, each young lady will receive six months of myrrh treatments. The other six months will be sweet perfumes and such.

He then closed the door and hurried along. I sighed with relief. Hegai seems like a friendly person, but he makes me feel rather uncomfortable.

I will write later, when I can!

Sincerely,

Esther

The Star: A Peek Inside Esther's Diary ♦ 47

12th day of Shevat
In the year of Jehovah
During the sixth year in the reign of King Xerxes

Dear Diary,

Today was much like the day before. As we did during previous days, the routine has been washing in the Women's Pool, being doused with myrrh, receiving massages, and other regal treatments.

In the midst of all these spa engagements, it can at times be difficult to find time to write. However, I can sometimes be able to write what I am thinking.

I see Mordecai frequently, for he often makes his way to our courtyard to see how I am doing. I really enjoy seeing my cousin, and talking with him makes me forget that I am still at a place other than my home. I asked him if he could bring Dan to my quarters.

He smiled and said, "I'd be glad to do so, my queen-to-be."

Then he bid me farewell, and turned back towards home. Now a servant is coming in with a platter of food. I must say goodbye.

Sincerely,

Esther

The Star: A Peek Inside Esther's Diary

>13th day of Shevat
>In the year of Jehovah
>During the sixth year in the reign of King Xerxes

Dear Diary,

Today Mordecai came to the courtyard with my dog, Dan! When Dan caught sight of me, he eagerly bounded from Mordecai's arms, and ran over to me. I picked him up, and cradled him in my arms.

I had asked Hegai if I could keep my dog with me, and thankfully he said that I could. My maidens have already set up a cozy little nook in my room for the dog.

I saw one girl wrinkle her eyebrows at the thought of having a dog in our living areas, but she continued to complete the task anyway. I have hope that she will change her mind once she meets my adorable, loving dog.

I thanked Mordecai and entered my room. I called to my maidens and proudly presented to them my dog.

Most of them seemed to ooh and aah over Dan. They were attracted to his charming disposition and his big beautiful brown eyes. They groomed his soft fur and rubbed his tummy. Dan rolled on the ground in delight. I think he really enjoyed all that attention.

After watching the excitement, Mordecai called goodbye and left to resume his duties in the king's court.

All too soon it was time for another beauty treatment, and my maidens hurried me along to another room to begin some more myrrh treatments.

I am resting on one of my ivory couches right now. The rest of today is pretty much to ourselves, so I have time to write. My maidens are still bustling around, dusting furniture, and attending to Dan, sewing new garments, or running errands.

It is very different being away from my home, living with Mordecai and Chana. I really miss spending time with them. Even though I detest sewing, I wish I were sewing with Chana beside the firepit right now.

Although I have all these comforts here, I feel that my childhood is over, and that the carefree days are behind me. I know that I am getting older, but I still have the heart of a child. I am saddened that life will not exactly be the same as it used to.

I feel that my childhood is over

But even despite my homesickness, I am still glad that Jehovah is with me. I am thankful that Jehovah has been blessing me and keeping me safe. It makes me wonder, with all of the things He has done for me, what other things He has up his sleeve.

Sincerely,

Esther

The Star: A Peek Inside Esther's Diary

15th day of Shevat
In the year of Jehovah
During the sixth year in the reign of Xerxes

Dear Diary,

Today is Yom Shabbat! I have personally requested of Hegai to have today off from receiving beauty treatments. He raised his eyebrow in surprise, but he obliged. I didn't tell him why because that would probably reveal my identity, and it is too dangerous to do so.

I have discovered that several of the girls, including Alzbeta and me, are Jews. So we each silently prayed, and tried our best to unnoticeably observe the Shabbat. The others who aren't Jews just continued to work.

I also read from a fragment of a scroll, which Mordecai brought to me one day when he visited my quarters. I am very happy that he did so, because I have longed for a scroll to read on Shabbat.

I will write later for I am going to continue reading the scroll.

Sincerely,

Esther

> One year later ...
> 20th day of Cheshvan
> In the year of Jehovah
> During the seventh year in the reign of King Xerxes

Dear Diary,

I am almost done with my perfume treatments, and soon I will see the king. I am quite relieved that my beauty session is almost up because all this pampering is getting sort of tiring.

So far, I have spent almost five complete months receiving perfume treatments. I have received many types of perfumes, some made of sweet prairie flowers, and some made of spices.

I have also spent time getting measured for different outfits. Because of all my maidens' hard work, my wardrobe is nearly bursting at the seams! It seems that every week, they start a new garment.

Although I can pick what I should wear for my appearance before the king, I entrusted Hegai to choose whatever garments he thinks are fitting. Today he came to look at my collection of clothes, but he shook his head. He said that none of them were exactly as beautiful as necessary, so he instructed them to make another one. He then gave a detailed description of what it should look like.

He chose pink satin material for my dress and a bright red for my headpiece. Immediately, my maidens set off to work. Since we only have a month until we must be seen before the king, they have to be as quick as possible.

I must write later, because it is time to be measured for a certain part of the garment.

Sincerely,

Esther

15th day of Kislev
In the year of Jehovah
During the seventh year in the reign of King Xerxes

Dear Diary,

The maidens are almost finished making my dress and veil. Now they are just adding the lace trim to the edge of my dress and adjusting the headpiece.

I am sort of excited about the day when I will appear before the king, but at the same time, the thought makes me nervous. I wonder what he will do when he sees me. Will he like me or reject me? I will never know until then.

Today Hegai explained to all of us contestants about the conduct that was expected from us. We were to be courteous and well-mannered. We were to carry ourselves confidently and look our very best and smile. I hope I am able to do all of those things when I come into the king's presence.

Sincerely,

Esther

The Star: A Peek Inside Esther's Diary ◆ 53

> 27th day of Kislev
> In the year of Jehovah
> During the seventh year of the reign of King Xerxes

Dear Diary,

I am now nearing the conclusion of my beauty treatments, and my appearance before King Xerxes is approaching.

The last plans are being made for the choosing of the new queen, and nearly everything is set in place. I observed streams of officials from other provinces flocking to see the event. It seemed that hundreds of people had come to spectate.

I have heard around the women's quarters that nearly all the inns in town are occupied, and many people have to seek shelter in the market square. Some even sleep in the outskirts of the forest. I normally do not like to be up front, observed by very curious onlookers, but I'll trust the Lord to help me, knowing that I am in His hands.

Sincerely,
Esther

6th day of Tevet
In the year of Jehovah
During the seventh year in the reign of King Xerxes

Dear Diary,

Today is the day before my appearance before the king. Since there have been so many virgins from throughout the different places in King Xerxes' empire, he is viewing them over several days.

> *The king will probably pick you*

Hegai came to my quarters today to examine the maidens' hard work. I could see by the grin on his face that he was very pleased. He congratulated them profusely. Then turning to me he said, "With your beautiful clothes and beautiful character, the king will probably pick you!"

Those words of encouragement eased my anxiety. Maybe it won't be so bad after all.

I must write later since I need to be well rested for my big day.

Sincerely,

Esther

The Star: A Peek Inside Esther's Diary ◆ 55

7th day of Tevet
In the year of Jehovah
During the seventh year in the reign of King Xerxes

Dear Diary,

I went before the king today. In a long procession of girls, I could feel stares following me. Everyone wanted to be seen as the most beautiful, and there was jealousy among us. But I didn't care what others thought about me. All that matters to me is that the Lord thinks I am beautiful, and His opinion is truly the one that matters.

When it was my turn to walk before the king, I walked boldly and smiled brightly. As soon as I reached the stairs that ascended to his royal throne, I bowed with my face nearly touching the floor. My heart pounded as I waited for the king's response. King Xerxes was impressed by my beauty. He called me nearer, and placed the heavy royal crown covered with many jewels on my head. Then he announced, "I hereby make you queen to replace Vashti."

> **I didn't care what others thought about me. All that matters to me is that the Lord thinks I am beautiful**

As I looked around at the faces looking at me, I spotted a couple of familiar faces, Mordecai and Chana; I smiled even more brightly. I could see that tears of joy glistened in Chana's eyes.

Then hurriedly, King Xerxes and I, as well as my maidens, were led to a large dining room. The king and I sat at the head of the table. Around us, the seats were quickly filled with chief advisors, princes, and governors. Soon the king's cupbearer brought in two glasses of wine for King Xerxes and me. Then dozens of other servants brought in enormous platters. I am well accustomed to be served with many delicacies, but this time they were even more savory and lots more of them. Several of the best calves in the king's herds had been prepared for the feast. There were baskets filled with many varieties of bread and a wide selection of fruits, such as figs and grapes.

I was quite filled, and I felt as though I had eaten enough for the whole week. I silently thanked God for continuing to bless me even more.

After a long feast, King Xerxes commanded his royal servants, Anidor and Atai to escort me, as well as my maidens, to a royal apartment alongside the palace. I had several luxurious rooms, a kitchen, reclining area, a bedroom, and rooms for the maidens, a large closet, and a dressing room. Soon Hegai and another man came carrying my bags of clothing and other items. I told my maidens that they could rest, and they soon all fell asleep.

I am content to be the queen, but at the same time I don't know if I will enjoy it. I have all the treasures that the empire can provide, but wonder if life will be as good as it seems right now. Will the king really love me, or will he only care about me for a little while? Will he be displeased that I don't worship his gods, or will he be tolerant of my beliefs? I guess I'll just have to find out.

Hegai told me while I was preparing to see the king that no one was permitted to enter before the king unless he has summoned them. You could be punished by death if you did!

I wonder if the king will ever call me. I hope he does one day.

Sincerely,
Esther, Queen of the Medo-Persian Empire

The Star: A Peek Inside Esther's Diary ◆ 57

*10th day of Tevet
In the year of Jehovah
During the seventh year in the reign of King Xerxes*

Dear Diary,

Today I went to visit Chana. I left very early in the morning before dawn. Hardly anyone was walking along the cobblestone streets as the city continued to rest. Two bodyguards accompanied me.

When I reached the doorsteps of the house, I knocked softly at the door. As I waited for Chana to open it, around me I could hear eerie sounds of the cool, misty morning. Finally, Chana opened the door. She was still wearing her nightcap and robe. She yawned, and motioned us inside.

She asked me tiredly, "What brings you here, my queen?"

"Sorry to disturb you at this time in the morning. I just came here to see how you and Mordecai are doing," I replied.

"Mordecai is upstairs getting ready to go to the palace. But he would probably be happy to see you before he leaves," Chana informed me.

When Mordecai came downstairs wearing his fancy robe and turban, he was surprised to see me once again standing in our living room. He greeted me cordially, and gave me a hug. Then after talking with us, he gave us a hasty farewell and dashed out the door.

I remained with Chana for a little while, and then told her I must leave. I said goodbye, and stepped out into the misty morning. Already the faint rays of the sun shone on the many buildings in the city. The city had little activity going on, but I noticed a few farmers trudging toward the city square to sell their goods. When they passed by me, they bowed and greeted me. I smiled in return. One particular little old man seemed to struggle to push his heavily laden cart filled with many fruits and vegetables. As I got closer, I realized it was

Sabba. We hugged each other and talked about his farm. He told me he is selling it to pay off debts. I was concerned about where he would live and prayed for him.

When I got back to the palace, my maidens greeted me as I walked into the room. They all gathered around me and asked me what I had been doing and numerous other questions. So for a good amount of time, the main room buzzed with chattering.

Finally, we started on our day, and the maidens began their daily duties. I also had mine to attend to as well.

I went to my private room and deeply engrossed myself in reading the latest news from other parts of the empire. I learned that a large aqueduct was being built in Egypt and there was an outbreak of fever in a small village in India. I also learned of new royalty being born, and other joyous occasions.

I am now in my room, writing peaceably.

Sincerely,

Esther, Queen of the Medo-Persian Empire

5th day of Shevat
In the year of Jehovah
During the seventh year in the reign of King Xerxes

Dear Diary,

As I was passing by the king's outer court, Mordecai noticed me, and called me to his side.

"Esther, he whispered, "There are two men, Bigthana and Teresh, who are quite upset with the king. They plan to kill him! You must let the king know right away!"

I alerted a nearby courier to take the important message to the king immediately. I told the servant to inform him that Mordecai was the one who found out their plot.

When the king received the message, he was quite grateful for it, but he had to deal with the two scoundrels. I heard him bellow to the guards to "seize the men and hang them on the gallows."

The soldiers hurried at once to obey his command. They busted through the heavy doors of the throne room and went to capture the two men. As they were led away, I heard the desperate cries of the men who had planned to harm the king.

Thanks to Mordecai, the king's life is spared. I'm sure that the king is quite relieved to escape the fate that would have been before him.

Sincerely,
Esther, Queen of the Medo-Persian Empire

> 15th day of Shevat
> In the year of Jehovah
> During the seventh year in the reign of King Xerxes

Dear Diary,

Today I went to the gardens. I laid on my back and gazed at the sky. I imagined that I could see the stars past the clouds and the mist. Up and away, free. It made me think suddenly of all the stars that never really have the chance to shine—because they are tucked away behind a curtain of status, rank, customs, and gender. It makes me sort of sad that when they accomplish the most, it happens at night when everyone is asleep. I am glad that I don't share that fate; perhaps I have some destiny that I will be remembered for. After all, that is what Mordecai told me as a little girl, so I suppose it is true. Perhaps I do have something to accomplish.

> *It made me think suddenly of all the stars that never really have the chance to shine*

This reminds me of a promise I made a long time ago to help all the little fallen stars regain their place and shine very abundantly! I must fulfill that promise. I must.

Finally, I walked down the road and found my way to the king's royal stable. When I first got married to him, he promised me that I could ride on one of his expensive purebred mares from Egypt. I had never taken the opportunity until today.

I rode around the palace grounds and the surrounding countryside. I really enjoyed myself because it gave me a break from all the formalities of being queen.

I patted the horse, and fed her an apple that I had in my apron. We took a rest for a while beside the pond. I sat under an oak tree and studied the little ants crawling in the dirt. They were building a new nest. As I watched the diligent ants, I suddenly remembered what King Solomon wrote long ago: "Go to the ant, you sluggard; consider its ways and be wise!" These were indeed wise creatures. They work together in such an amazing way. It makes me think that since humans are much more intelligent than ants, we should work together even more than we do now!

When I got home, I had dinner. After I took my bath and brushed my hair, I settled down on my bed and decided to write a little bit. Well, my candle is running out. Goodnight.

Sincerely,

Esther, Queen of the Medo-Persian Empire

> Three years later …
> 14th day of Nissan
> In the year of Jehovah
> During the eleventh year in the reign of King Xerxes

Dear Diary,

Today there was an announcement of the promotion of Haman. He is now second in command of the kingdom! I have seen him before, and it seems to me that he is a proud and boastful man.

I went to the palace outer court today to visit Mordecai. In his little office, he was busily writing. He waved when he saw me and then returned to work. After a while, Mordecai stood up and stretched.

"I'm going to take a walk in the courtyard," he told me.

The two of us walked out into the courtyard, and separated. As I turned away, I saw Haman. As he walked through the courtyard, all the servants bowed down before him. Everyone that is, except for Mordecai.

Haman frowned. I guess his pride was hurt because he pouted as he strolled away and seemed to struggle to keep his composure.

Sincerely,

Esther, Queen of the Medo-Persian Empire

The Star: A Peek Inside Esther's Diary ◆ 63

23rd day of Nissan
In the year of Jehovah
During the eleventh year in the reign of King Xerxes

Dear Diary,

Today I joined some workers as they made oil. It took several bucketfuls of olives and grapes. I got a lot of exercise from walking back and forth from the house and to the orchard.

They dumped all the olives into a barrel. Using a long stick, they pounded the olives, until the mixture gradually became thin enough. It took a long time to pound them. I helped with the pounding a little, and I enjoyed it!

Some of the maidens went to town to walk around afterwards, but others lagged behind and talked together. Here I am now, reclining on my bed as I write. In here it is more peaceful and quiet. It feels good to have time alone in my room. I have spent some time with Jehovah, and I read from Father's scroll. I love to read it whenever I can.

I will write later. Good night!

Sincerely,

Esther, queen of the Medo-Persian Empire

> One year later...
> 15th day of Sivan
> In the year of Jehovah
> During the twelfth year in the reign of King Xerxes

Dear Diary,

Today my maidens told me that my cousin Mordecai was in great distress about something. They had seen him in sackcloth and his head sprinkled with ashes.

One of them told me all about the plan to annihilate all of the Jews. This is what made Mordecai so upset. I was told that Mordecai wants me to go before the king to plead for the Jews! Me? Unbelievable! Was Mordecai unaware of the fate that could await a person if they went before the king without permission?

I instantly sent back a message to Mordecai explaining the fact that I haven't been called for and that my chances were quite slim if I appeared before the king.

But Mordecai responded with the message that if I didn't take action, maybe someone else would and save the Jews, but I would perish. Because I live on the palace grounds doesn't mean that I am exempt from being annihilated. He ended with the thought that maybe God had a reason for me being queen.

Although my heart pounded with fear, and a mob of butterflies filled my stomach, I responded to Mordecai, that I would do it. I urged him and all the Jews to pray and fast for three days, and then I would go before the king. If the king grants me pardon, or if he kills me, I accept it.

I hope Jehovah will help His people during this dangerous time!

Sincerely,

Esther, Queen of the Medo-Persian Empire

The Star: A Peek Inside Esther's Diary ◆ 65

16th day of Sivan
In the year of Jehovah
During the twelfth year in the reign of Xerxes

Dear Diary,

Today has been quite another solemn day. Even the beautiful sun shining doesn't lift the gloom that the Jews experience.

My eyes are red from crying nearly all morning. I have been earnestly praying for Jehovah to work a miracle, and for strength to do the task ahead of me.

This is a very overwhelming and stressful situation, but through it all, I am trying to continue to trust in Jehovah during this difficult time. Fear seems take hold of me, and anxiety grips me. I can't seem to shake loose of it.

As the day nears in which I will go before the king, I have grown even more nervous. I have noticed that most of my maidens have now chosen to accept Jehovah as their God, so I am not alone in my anguish.

I continue to pray to Jehovah. Maybe He has other good things in store.

Sincerely,
Esther, Queen of the Medo-Persian Empire

22nd day of Sivan
In the year of Jehovah
During the twelfth year in the reign of King Xerxes

Dear Diary,

This morning I was up quite early. I had a bad dream of the twelve stars from Joseph's dream long ago, slowly disappearing and fading away. One by one, the stars disintegrated, and I could hear desperate cries of humans as they were being destroyed. I happened to be on one of those stars, along with Mordecai and Chana. I could feel the star shaking and slowly crumbling. Then Mordecai and Chana started to fall, I screamed and reached over the edge and tried to save them, but to no avail. Then I felt the star tilt, and I slowly lost my balance and plunged into the darkness below.

Terrified I woke up. I couldn't go back to sleep. I wrung my hands and paced back and forth in my room. I couldn't bear to think of innocent women and children being killed without cause. My family, my friends, my people, and maybe even my God would seem to become a thing of the past. It would also greatly devastate the royal family. King Xerxes had several concubines who were of Jewish decent, and bore him children. Some of his own children would be slaughtered!

From that experience I knew that I really had to do something, even if I have to risk my life. I must reveal the person behind it all. So I got myself together and prayed intensely.

Now I must get going, because the king is probably in the courtroom by now. May Jehovah be with me.

Sincerely,

Esther, Queen of the Medo-Persian Empire

The Star: A Peek Inside Esther's Diary ◆ 67

Afternoon

I am surprisingly still alive! Praise the Lord! King Xerxes did something that is not usually done in the Medo-Persian Empire.

I nervously tiptoed into the glorious throne room. The king was sitting on his throne, embroiled in an argument with an officer. He didn't appear happy at all, and I was quite afraid to go near him. It felt that at any second his anger could strike me down like a bolt

I am surprisingly still alive!

of lightning, but nevertheless I continued to walk down the aisle leading to the massive golden throne. However, I didn't go long without being unnoticed. Soon, King Xerxes spotted me. He smiled and called me forward, holding out the golden scepter. Relief flooded me as I bowed before him and touched the golden scepter. What a change in attitude! His anger seemed to have just magically disappeared.

He asked me what I wanted and told me that half of his kingdom was mine if I but asked. I nervously asked if he and Haman would like to come to my quarters for dinner tonight. The king was surprised, but accepted the invitation.

I put together the menu and chose the tablecloth and plates and other things that we used. My maidens dusted the furniture, cleaned the vases, and put everything back in order, while Magdalene and several other maidens started to prepare the food.

Finally every little detail was taken care of, and the hour that the king and Haman were to arrive drew nearer. I went to my closet, and selected a light blue dress, with a hem that was embroidered with floral designs. The garment is elegant, but simple.

Soon the king arrived. King Xerxes and Haman were ushered into my quarters. As I caught sight of the king, I bowed before him and led him and Haman to their reserved places. The king seemed pleased as he walked onto the porch decorated so lavishly in his honor. Haman followed behind the king.

The king gazed in awe as more food was added to the already full table. He particularly enjoyed the roasted lamb, which was prepared with special spices and herbs. Haman and the king talked and laughed and overall had a pleasant time. I made sure that there was just enough food for them at all times. Finally, wine was brought in. I had requested that grape juice be served instead of the traditional brainwashing Persian wine that was usually served at such a lavish feast. The king didn't seem to notice much that the "wine" was not truly wine.

Haman and the king toasted. After they clanked their golden goblets, the king drank the juice quickly. After a while, the men finally seemed to notice that I was sitting at the table. The king said it was a wonderful feast! As he inquired of my request, he again said that he would give up even half of my kingdom to me, his precious queen!

I asked him to come back to dinner tomorrow night and I would have my petition.

I dictated a letter to Mordecai and sent it with one of my maidens. Today, I feel was one of the most important days of my life. I'm getting rather sleepy now, so goodnight.

Sincerely,

Esther, Queen of the Medo-Persian Empire

The Star: A Peek Inside Esther's Diary ◆ 69

19th day of Nissan
In the year of Jehovah
During the twelfth year in the reign of King Xerxes

Dear Diary,

Earlier in the day

Today we decided to have a light brunch in the king's royal gardens.

We placed blankets, home woven from sturdy material, unpacked our lunch and ate as we enjoyed the beauty around us.

After a while, we saw a long processional on the main road of Susa following a man leading a horse whose rider was dressed in elaborate robes. The man on the royal horse was my own cousin, Mordecai! He was being paraded around town dressed like a king with Haman leading him throughout the city. I'm sure I saw Haman with a scowl across his face barely covered with a fake smile. The parade moved on, and the garden and surrounding area grew silent again.

We left and came home to prepare for the king who will arrive any moment now so I must finish getting ready. Goodbye!

After the feast

The king came around two o'clock with Haman and a few bodyguards. I greeted them and seated them at a long table in my dining hall instead of outside on the porch. Haman and the king both reclined on ivory couches with scarlet blankets draped over the side. I reclined on the opposite side of the table facing Haman and the king.

Before long, the food was brought on trays. The king had a large portion of roasted quail, which kept him busy for a while. Surprisingly, he also enjoyed the lentil soup, which was simple, but quite filling. Haman also had his huge helpings of food. Between mouthfuls of food, the king and Haman engaged in a discussion about politics. I remained quiet and listened until the king asked me for my opinion on the matter. That, too, was odd. The king was in such a pleasant mood. Eventually, he turned to me and asked what I wanted.

I silently said a quick prayer and mustered up my courage. I pleaded with him on behalf of my people. I told him that we were to be murdered—young and old, women and children included.

He asked, "Who would have dared to plot such an evil plan to rid me of my queen—and her people?" His voice was filled with deep rage.

> *This man, Haman, is the one!*

I pointed at Haman. "This man, Haman, is the one! He hates my cousin, Mordecai, and has planned to harm him as well as all my people!"

The king became enraged and asked Haman to explain.

Haman, still in shock, came to me and knelt before me begging me to save his life.

Immediately the king's bodyguards, who seemed to be asleep until then, rushed to the scene. Picking Haman up they chained him hand and foot, draped his head with his outer robe that rested on the couch, and dragged him out of the room. He struggled to get free from their grip, but to no avail. At the king's command, the bodyguards took Haman out to the gallows and hanged him. Haman's own gallows that he had built to hang Mordecai on. Sad irony.

It is now almost sunset, so I better get some rest. This has been an emotional day. Goodbye for now.

Sincerely,

Esther, Queen of the Medo Persian Empire

24th day of Sivan
In the year of Jehovah
During the twelfth year in the reign of King Xerxes

Dear Diary,

Yesterday I went to talk with the king, and a new decree was made overwriting Haman's wicked plot! The Jews are now able to protect themselves from their enemies and plunder the houses of their conquered adversaries, just like Haman planned to happen to us! God is indeed faithful. The scribes stayed up all night making copies of the new decree to take to all 127 provinces. A number of the couriers left early this morning. While I was still in my bed, I heard the clopping of horse's hooves, and I didn't get that much rest!

Sincerely,

Esther, Queen of the Medo-Persian Empire

The Star: A Peek Inside Esther's Diary

>29th day of Sivan
>In the year of Jehovah
>During the twelfth year in the reign of King Xerxes

Dear Diary,

Today is the day that was scheduled for our doom.

Our people are now safe! No Jewish blood has been spilled or property has been lost. Praise Jehovah! I am so overjoyed! God is truly amazing! No one even came on our property. Everywhere you can hear shouts of praise and thanksgiving.

I went to see the king because he had summoned me to tell me the good news. He reported that 500 of the Jews' enemies had been killed including Haman's ten sons.

Mordecai suggested that we should order a national holiday for the Jews to remind them of this day!

Sincerely,

Esther, Queen of the Medo-Persian Empire

13th day of Adar
In the year of Jehovah
During the twelfth year in the reign of King Xerxes

Dear Diary,

Ever since I went to live with my cousin Mordecai and his wife, Chana, I've been called "Esther." Most people, however, don't realize my birth name is "Hadassah," which means "myrtle." Mother had told me that she and Father decided on that name since my birth brought them the sweetness of a flower during a really bitter time. It was also given because myrtle trees are very beautiful.

During these last few days I've thought about "Hadassah" even more and realized how it isn't too different from "Esther." Myrtles brighten nature kind of like stars. The days before the king's new decree were very bitter for all of us. Now things have become even sweeter as our survival is actually becoming a reality.

I also think about what Mordecai said about my name "Esther." He said that I would one day be a star. I never really understood what he meant until I had to shine. However, when I did, I could almost see the slight twinkle of many stars all across Susa, gradually growing brighter and brighter. I could almost touch and feel the myrtles starting to bud even before daylight.

Jehovah surely did have a special job for me, once an ordinary peasant and an orphan. He called me to serve in ways I never imagined, to be a flower and a star, for such a time as this.

Sincerely,
Esther, Queen of the Medo Persian Empire

TEACH Services, Inc.
P U B L I S H I N G

We invite you to view the complete
selection of titles we publish at:
www.TEACHServices.com

We encourage you to write us
with your thoughts about this,
or any other book we publish at:
info@TEACHServices.com

TEACH Services' titles may be purchased in
bulk quantities for educational, fund-raising,
business, or promotional use.
bulksales@TEACHServices.com

Finally, if you are interested in seeing
your own book in print, please contact us at:
publishing@TEACHServices.com
We are happy to review your manuscript at no charge.

www.ingramcontent.com/pod-product-compliance
Lightning Source LLC
Chambersburg PA
CBHW042133160426
43199CB00021B/2903